Luigi Bordèse

# The Rose of Savoy

Operetta for ladies

Luigi Bordèse

**The Rose of Savoy**
*Operetta for ladies*

ISBN/EAN: 9783337314569

Printed in Europe, USA, Canada, Australia, Japan

Cover: Foto ©Thomas Meinert / pixelio.de

More available books at **www.hansebooks.com**

Luigi Bordèse

**The Rose of Savoy**
*Operetta for ladies*

ISBN/EAN: 9783337314569

Printed in Europe, USA, Canada, Australia, Japan

Cover: Foto ©Thomas Meinert / pixelio.de

More available books at **www.hansebooks.com**

# The Rose of Savoy

## OPERETTA FOR LADIES

Words by
### H. B. FARNIE

Music by
### LUIGI BORDESE

Adapted and Revised by M. C. J.

## OLIVER DITSON COMPANY

BOSTON, 453-463 Washington St.     LONDON, 192 High Holborn, W. C.

New York
C. H. DITSON & CO.
867 Broadway.

Chicago
LYON & HEALY
Cor. Wabash Ave. and Adams St.

Boston
JOHN C. HAYNES & CO.
33 Court and 453 Washington St.

Philadelphia
J. E. DITSON & Co.
1228 Chestnut St.

# CHARACTERS.

CATARINA ( *Prima donna* ) . . . . . . . . . . 1st Soprano.
JACQUELINE ( *A Savoyard flower girl* ) . . . . . . . Contralto.
MISS CHIPPINS, ( *A milliner and dressmaker* ) . . . . 2d Soprano.

*Chorus of young girls, modistes in the shop of* MISS CHIPPINS.

---

# SCENE.

The workroom of MISS CHIPPIN'S shop in New York. The time is after sunset. Two tables are ranged down the room, one at each side, leaving a wide avenue between. On these tables lie dresses, etc. One or two robes are hung up on stands. The usual paraphernalia of a modiste's shop lie about.

If there is a curtain, MISS CHIPPINS and her girls are discovered at work when it rises; if there is not, they must enter by a side door, bearing dresses, wreaths, etc., and seat themselves at their work-tables. One side door, which is supposed to lead to the front shop and to the street, is sufficient. A window at back is an advantage. The characters enter immediately after the overture is finished.

---

# COSTUMES.

CATARINA wears a rich ball dress; JACQUELINE a gay Savoyard dress, made short. She bears a basket of flowers, and should have her face a little browned. Colored crayons will do this well. MISS CHIPPINS is an elderly lady, and should have her hair dusted with powder ( or flour ), and wear spectacles. The chorus should wear gay dresses,— colored muslins, etc.

---

*Time of representation, 35 minutes.*

(2)

# THE ROSE OF SAVOY.

## OPERETTA.

### OVERTURE.

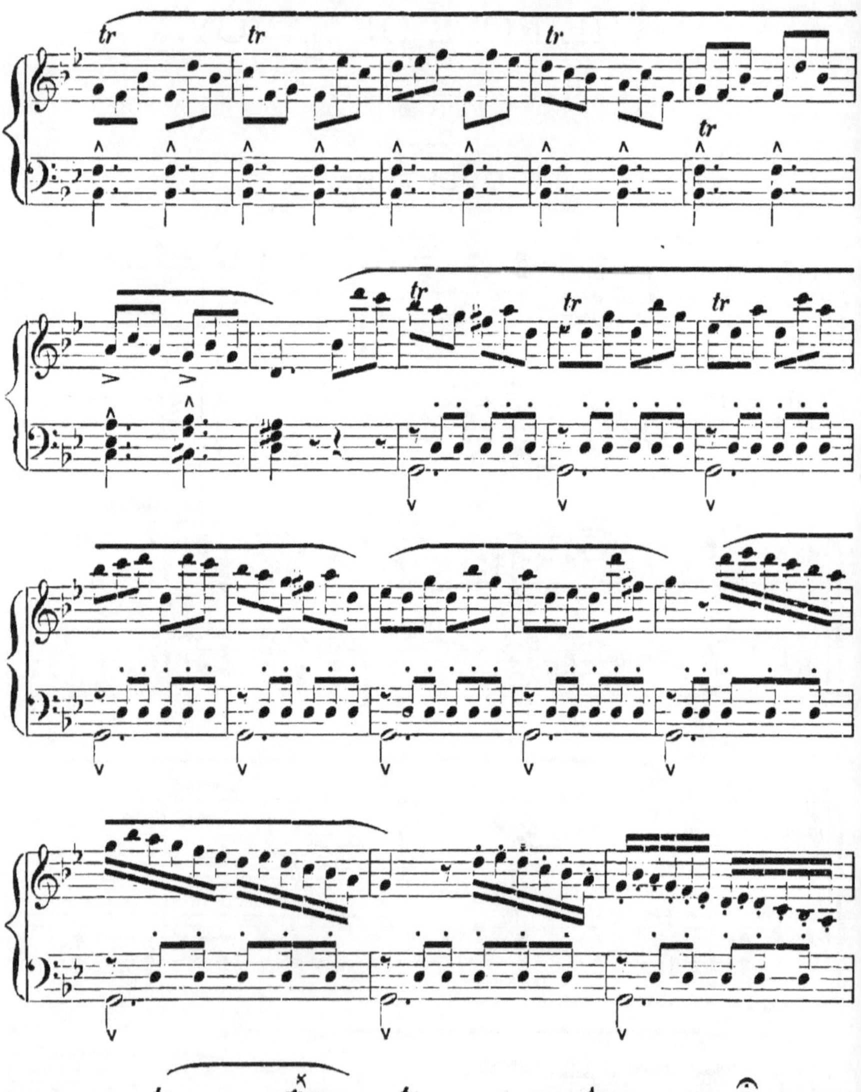

_Allegro con grazia._

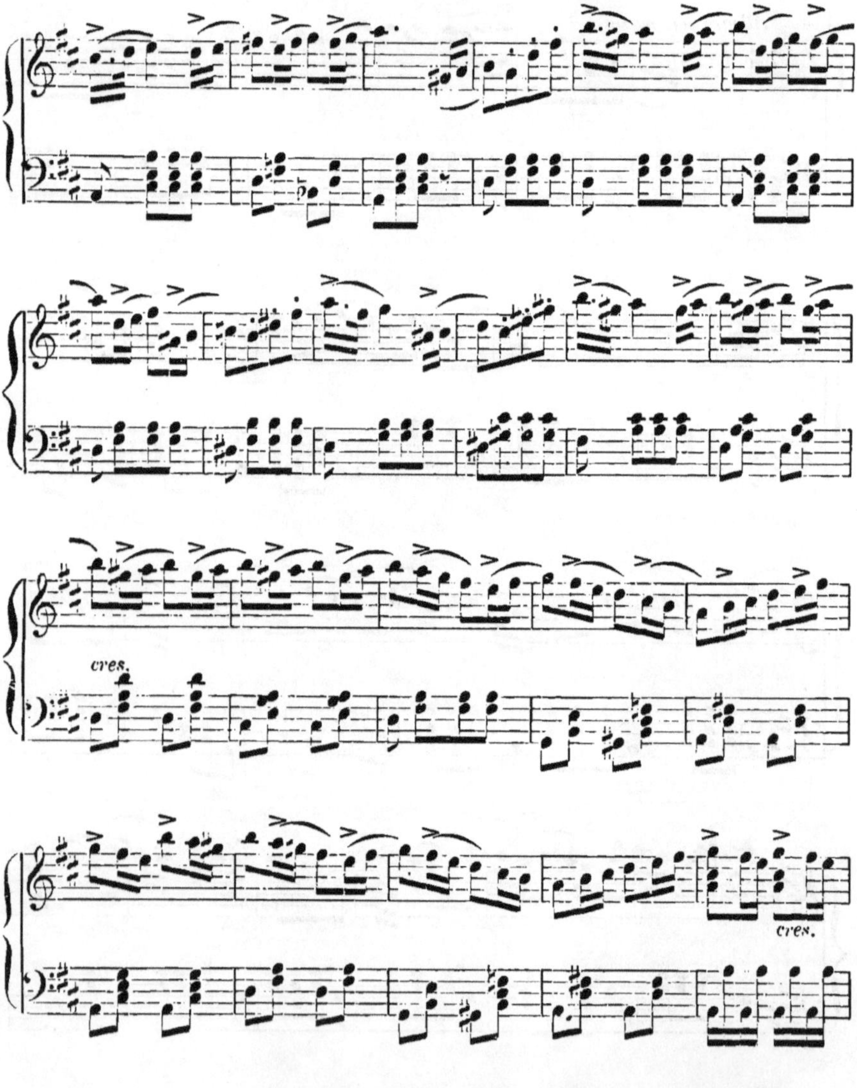
cres.
cres.
ff

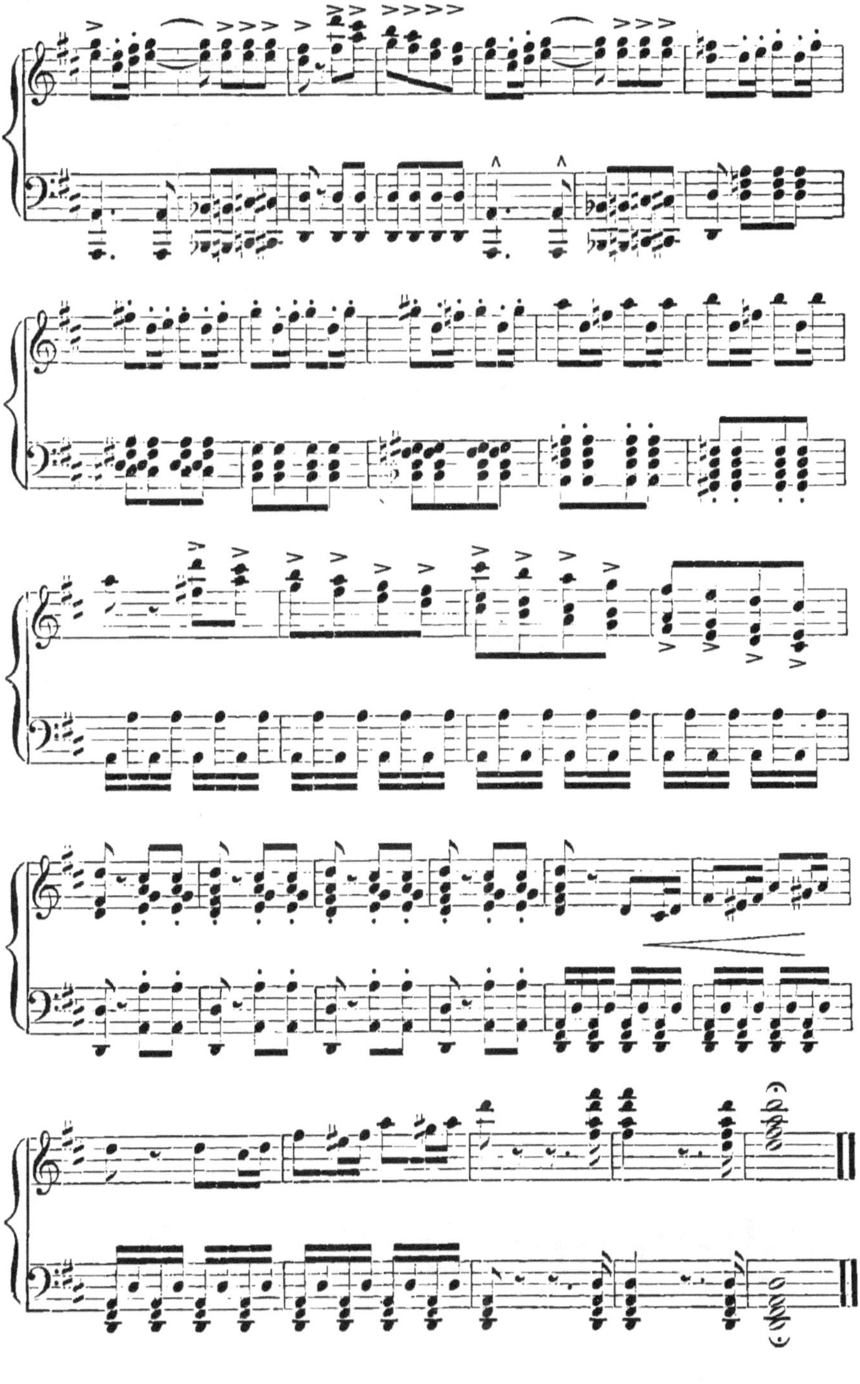

# No. 1. SISTERS STILL WE ARE BUSY.

## CHORUS AND SOLO.

*(Miss Chippins and her girls, making artificial wreaths, finishing dresses, etc.)*
*Allegro moderato.*

MISS CHIPPENS AND FIRST SOPRANO.

Sis - ters, still we are bu - sy sew - ing, Tho' the

SECOND SOPRANO.

Sis - ters, still we are bu - sy sew - ing, Tho' the

day - light hath left the hours, And on sat - in and silk field

day - light hath left the hours, And on sat - in and sil' field

grow-ing, Bloom all brightly our broi-der'd flow'rs! What with work-ing, what with

*mf*

grow-ing, Bloom all brightly our broi-der'd flow'rs! What with work-ing, what with

*mf*

*mf*

sing -ing Le - gend wild of old - en time, On swift pin - ions night is

sing - ing Le - gend wild of old - en time, On swift pin - ions night is wing - ing, To the eve - ning bells' soft chime! . . . sil - ver

wing - ing, To the eve - ning bells' soft chime! . . .

chime, . . . . sil - ver chime, . . . . To the eve - ning bells' soft

sil - ver chime, sil - ver chime, eve - ning bells' soft

chime! Sis - ters, still we are bu - sy sew - ing, Tho' the

chime! Sis - ters, still we are bu - sy sew - ing, Tho' the

day - light hath left    the    hours, . . . And on   sat - in and silk   field

day - light hath left    the    hours, . . . And on   sat - in and silk   field

grow - ing,    Bloom all   bright - ly  our broi - der'd  flow'rs!    And    in

grow - ing,    Bloom all   bright - ly  our broi - der'd  flow'rs!    And    in

sat - in and silk   field   grow - ing, Bloom   all   bright-ly  our broi - der'd

sat - in and silk   field   grow - ing, Bloom   all   bright-ly  our broi - der'd flow'rs!    bright - ly bloom,    bright - ly bloom,    bright - ly

flow'rs!    bright - ly bloom,    bright - ly bloom,    bright - ly

bloom    our    flow'rs!    As   we sew,

bloom    our    flow'rs!    As   we sew,

there they grow, . . . our bloom - ing flow'rs!    As   we sew,

there they grow, . . . our bloom - ing flow'rs!    As   we sew, there they grow, our blooming flow'rs! As we sew, there they bloom and

there they grow, our blooming flow'rs! As we sew, there they bloom and

*cres. sempre.*

grow! As we sew, there they bloom and grow! . . . . . .

grow! As we sew, there they bloom and grow! . . . . . .

FINE.

FINE.

Poco meno mosso. MISS CHIPPENS. (SOLO.)

Li - lies white . . for pale and thoughtful maid - en, Ro - ses red . . . for charms that darkly glow. . .

La - dies! when your bra - ver - y ar-ray'd in, One grace more . . to us you sure - ly owe! Yes! surely you owe! Yes! sure-ly you owe! . .

D.S. as full chorus. All voices.

rit.

Miss Chippins. Now, girls, how are you getting on with the Signorina's wreath? She will be sure to be here soon. For you must know she appears to-night at the theater in a new opera, and woe to us poor milliners if all her dress be not ready.

1st Girl. Ah! Miss Chippins, we have been working so hard! See, the wreath is almost done. (*Holds it up.*)

2d Girl. And I only want to put a few more stitches to this lovely belt.

3d Girl. I wish I were a *prima donna?* Heigh ho! (*Yawns.*)

All the Girls. So do I!

Miss Chippins. Quiet, little chatterboxes; you really don't know what you are saying. Proud is the position of Catarina, no doubt, and I can quite understand you envying her a little; but you do not know the toil and anxiety she has doubtless experienced before coming to what she is.

1st Girl. Tell us Catarina's history, Miss Chippins.

All the Girls. Yes! do tell us!

Miss Chippins. Oh, I would if I could; but I really don't know any more about it than yourselves.

2d Girl. For my part, I think she is a very proud and haughty personage.

3d Girl. No well-born lady would flounce in and out the way she does, and speak us if we were so many bits of machinery!

Miss Chippins. Peace, you gossips! Did anybody ever hear such scandal! and of such a good customer, too, as Catarina! (*Clock strikes seven.*) Seven o'clock! Thank goodness, we are well forward with our work,—so the Signorina can come when she likes. How dark it is! Let us have the candles lit!

(1st Girl *goes out and returns with lighted candles.*)

1st Girl. Well, for me, I rather like twilight,—so poetical.

2d Girl. So suggestive of ghosts,—I like ghosts!

All the Girls. Oh, don't say so! Dreadful!

3d Girl. Do you believe in ghosts, Miss Chippins?

Miss Chippins. Why, not exactly. But I confess I like the old goblin stories of my childhood—that imagine spirits in the fire, and in the air, and on the dreary moor.

All the Girls. O, tell us some legend, Miss Chippins.

Miss Chippins. Well! If you're very quiet I'll sing you an old ballad, which admonishes us to pray against all unholy influences.

## No. 2. WHEN ALL THE STILL HOUSE SLUMBERS.

### BALLAD.

*Andante moderato.* Miss Chippins. p

1. When all the still house slumbers, And the
2. When 'mid the tem - pest glooming, Streaming

p *Misterioso.*

wan-ing stars expire, And peals its sol-emn num - bers The dim ca-the-dral
light'nings wildly play, And thunders, loud-ly boom - ing, The hearts of men dis-

*marcato.*

*rit.*

*Allegro vivo.*

spire! The dim ca-the-dral spire! On roof-tree and on raft-er,
may, The hearts of men dis-may. When rain tor-rents are lash-ing,

*soave.* ff p

Flut-ter a phan-tom crew; And groans, shrieking and laughter, Shud-der the still-ness
Ghosts are a-bout be sure, On lone-ly trav-'lers dash-ing Lost on the dark-ling

ff p

through! Then pray .. so that the spi-rits work no harm, Else they may
moor. Then pray .. so that the spi-rits work no harm, Else they may

ff p

weave ma-ny a wick-ed charm. Then pray, so that they work no harm

Pray, so that they work no harm, no harm. . . . . . . . . . . .

D. C. for 2d verse.

ALL THE GIRLS. Thanks! thanks! How very good of you!

3d GIRL. Well, I must say, I think people only see ghosts when they've had too much supper.

2d GIRL. Dreadful idea! But *you're* not at all romantic.

MISS CHIPPINS. All the better, perhaps.

1st GIRL. Don't you think, Miss Chippins, that imagination has its uses? We should become melancholy if we could not build up little castles in the air, and fill them with phantoms, or —

3d GIRL. Phantoms!

2d GIRL. Or great ladies!

ALL THE GIRLS. Or dukes with titles!

MISS CHIPPINS. There is a wonderful charm in fancy. The danger is that you indulge in nonsense. Still, I would not have you without a scrap of imagination about you, it would injure business! Hark! what is that — music?

(*The symphony to next song is begun very softly.* 1st GIRL *runs to window and looks out.*)

1st GIRL. Oh! Miss Chippins, 't is the strange flower-girl, Jacqueline, who so often sings in our street!

MISS CHIPPINS. Hush! She is beginning. Let us listen.

(JACQUELINE *sings the first verse of her song behind the scenes, then enters, comes forward, and sings second verse.*)

## No. 3.    FROM FAIR SAVOY I COME.

### ROMANCE AND CHORUS.

JACQUELINE (*behind the scene*).

From fair Sa - voy I come, Whose hills are gemm'd with snow, And

sell - ing these poor flow'rs, Thro' all the world I go! Rich la - dies oft I

see, Still do I not re - pine, Con - tent their lot should

be, More bright and gay than mine, More bright and gay, more gay than

*Allegretto.*

mine... A mi - ser yet am I, .... For I hoard .. up my

lit - tle store, And when I'm rich I'll go . . . To my own . . fa-ther-

land once more! Once more, once more, once more, once

more, ............... once more, once more.

MISS CHIPPINS AND GIRLS.

She loves her na - tive land, . . And she hoards . . up her scan-ty store That

She loves her na - tive land, . . And she hoards . . up her scan-ty store That

*p*

so when she is rich, . . . She may go . . . . to Sa-voy once more, once

so when she is rich, . . . She may go . . . . to Sa-voy once more, once

JACQUELINE.

Once more,    once more,    once more,         once more,      once

MISS CHIPPINS AND GIRLS.

more,    once more,    once more,    once  more,         once more,

more,    once more,    once more,    once  more,         once more,

*ff*                              (JACQUELINE *enters.*)

more,    once more,    once  more! . . . . . . . . . . .

once more,    once more, once  more! . . . . . . . . . .

once more,    once more, once  more! . . . . . . . . . .

*ff*

JACQUELINE.

2. How sweet, how fresh my flow'rs, Just gath-ered from the dell, The

*p*

dews of morn still lurk, With - in each ti - ny cell! But soon, a - las! their

bloom, Will with - er and de - cay, And I, far from my

*rit.*

home, Will fade as fast as they, as fast as they, as fast as

*Allegretto.*

they! . . A mi - ser yet am I, . . . . For I hoard . . up my

lit - tle store, And when I'm rich I'll go . . . To my own . . fa-ther-

land once more! Once more, once more, once more, once

more, . . . . . . . . . . . . . . . . once more, once more!

*ff*

MISS CHIPPINS AND GIRLS.

She loves her na - tive land . . And she hoards . . up her scan - ty store, That

She loves her na - tive land . . And she hoards . . up her scan - ty store, That

so when she is rich, . . . She may go . . . . to Sa-voy once more, once

so when she is rich, . . . She may go . . . . to Sa-voy once more, once

JACQUELINE.

Once more, once more, once more, once more, once

MISS CHIPPINS AND GIRLS.

more, once more, once more, once more, once more,

more, once more, once more, once more, once more,

*ff*

more, once more, once more! . . . . . . . . . . .

once more, once more, once more! . . . . . . . . . . .

once more, once more, once more! . . . . . . . . . . .

*ff*

MISS CHIPPINS. So, you have come again, Jacqueline! But why call yourself a miser, as you do in your song?

JACQUELINE. Only a miser, madam, for my country's sake; for the sake of once more treading the joyous hills of old Savoy, and re-living the happy past.

MISS CHIPPINS. And you save up all your money for that?

JACQUELINE. All that I can put by.

MISS CHIPPINS. And how much have you saved up to the present, Jacqueline?

JACQUELINE. Half a dollar!

1st GIRL. Oh, Miss Chippins, what a sum to travel with! Why, I have more in my purse just now!

MISS CHIPPINS. You 'll not have it very long!

2d GIRL. Yes, let us make a contribution to add to poor Jacqueline's little home-fund.

1st GIRL. Yes, let us. I 'll carry round the plate.

2d GIRL. Wait till the middle of the service!

MISS CHIPPINS (to 1st GIRL.) Go and accomplish your charitable design!

1st GIRL (takes round her work-basket and solicits contributions, saying): For the poor Savoyard flower-girl, if you please, (to MISS CHIPPINS).

MISS CHIPPINS (dropping coin into basket). With pleasure!

2d GIRL. Here goes the Sunday School cent.

( Drops it into basket. )

3d GIRL. Here is mine! Come on, all of you!

( They each drop a coin into the basket.)

1st GIRL. And here is mine. So, Jacqueline, a trifling addition to your patriotic fund.

( Gives her the money.)

JACQUELINE. Oh, ladies, how good you are! Why, with this, and what my flowers bring me, in the course of two or three years I shall have enough to pay my way home again. But you must have some flowers! You won't? Ah, you have no need! You wear already the roses in your cheeks, and the lilies in your pure lives. Thanks! now I am indeed happy!

( Exit, singing merrily. The girls set to work, softly humming the music of first chorus. )

MISS CHIPPINS. Now, girls, hasten on with the prima donna's wreath. She will be here soon.

1st GIRL. My work is completed.

2d GIRL. And mine.

MISS CHIPPINS. All in good time. ( Bell rings.) And there is the prima donna!

( Enter CATARINA. The girls rise to receive her.)

CATARINA. Good day, ladies. I hope my dress is ready. Not ready? Oh, really, this is too bad.

2d GIRL ( to her companions ). Didn't I say she was a proud thing?

MISS CHIPPINS (to CATARINA). Pardon, madam, the dress is perfectly ready, and the wreath, and the bouquet. And, you will allow me to add, they are perfection.

( The girls bring them forward.)

CATARINA. They are indeed — charming! How well you have worked, and all to such good purpose! Your labor, young ladies, is indeed a science, and you exalt it into an art.

1st GIRL (to 2d). She proud! I call her charming!

2d GIRL. Wait till she sees the bill!

CATARINA. Your rivalry of Nature in these flowers should make her jealous!

MISS CHIPPINS. You will make my girls proud, madam. Nature, who gives the finest of all flowers, is not proud, for that reason.

CATARINA. Ah, but you have made this dress so well, I must do something for you in return. Say, young ladies, would you care to go to the opera to-night and admire your handiwork?

MISS CHIPPINS. Impossible, Donna Catarina; we are too busy, and must work through the small hours.

1st GIRL. But, please, signora — ( hesitates ).

MISS CHIPPINS. Well? Speak!

1st GIRL. Though we can 't go to hear the

Donna Catarina — we — we (*to* 2d GIRL) Oh, you tell her what we would like!

2d GIRL. Why, Miss Chippins, if the lady would sing for us here, it would be almost as good as going to the opera, (*aside*) and four dollars cheaper!

ALL THE GIRLS. Yes, that's it! Do sing!

CATARINA. Sing for you? Oh, with pleasure,

if you wish it. What shall it be? I appear to-night in the new opera, "The Mariner's Daughter." If you like, I will sing you the Cavatina.

ALL THE GIRLS. Oh, thanks, madam.

3d GIRL. I call her the most affable lady I ever knew!

2d GIRL. You talk too much!

## No. 4. THE MARINER'S DAUGHTER.

*Agitato.*
CATARINA. (RECIT.) **RECITATIVE AND AIR.**

A - las! he com - eth not! my heart is nigh des -

*ppp trem.*

pair - ing! O will he 'scape with life from that sea rag - ing

wild! My fa - ther 'gainst the waves what a - vail - eth thy

*f*

*Lento.*

dar - ing? Ah! nev - er - more wilt thou come to thy child!

*Lento.*

*Andantino.*

Am I then

left on earth all lone - ly, Want-ing thy kind pro-tect - ing

care? In Par - a - dise my moth - er dwell - eth; Hast thou then gone to join her there, to join her there? Nev-er a-gain thy white sail

watch - ing, As it toss'd o'er the har - bor bar, Shall I strain

ear and heart to lis - ten For thy dear voice when yet a -

*Agitato molto.*

far! Ne'er shall I strain mine ear to lis-ten, For thy dear voice while still afar! Am I then

*Agitato molto.*

left on earth all lone - ly, Wanting thy kind pro - tect - ing

care? In Par'a - dise my moth - er dwell - eth; Hast thou then

*a piacere.*

gone to join her there, to join her there, to join her there?

*Quasi a piacere imitando un canto lontano.*

What

*Allegro vivo.*

hear I? 'tis my fa-ther! 'Tis his voice sound - ing nigh! Then Heav'n . . . in mer-cy great Hath heard my anx - - - - - - ious cry! Hath heard my anx - ious cry!

*Allegro con grazio.*

O moment of rap - ture! my

fa - ther is near,    O heart, calm thy beat - ing, And no lon - ger

fear!      My fa - ther is near;    O heart, calm thy

beat-ing, And no long - er fear! From storm and from tempest, He 's safe by my

side, No more to brave death, On the rude o-cean wide! No more to brave

death, On the rude o - cean wide! Ah! . . . . . . . . . . . . . . . .

. . . . . . . . . Ah! . . . . . . . . . . . O mo-ment of

rap - ture! My fa - ther is near; O heart, calm thy beat-ing, And

no long-er fear! O heart, calm thy beat - ing, And no long-er

fear! O heart,...... heart,...... heart! no long - er

fear! O calm thy beat - ing, heart, calm .. thy

*Piu mosso.*

*ff*

beat - - - - ing,      heart!

Calm ... thy beat - - - - ing, . . . . . . . .

... Calm thy beat-ing, no long-er fear!

(*At the close they throw at her feet the artificial flowers from their work-baskets, crying, "Brava!" and applauding. At this moment* JACQUELINE *appears at the entrance.*)

MISS CHIPPINS. Why, here is the Savoyard again. Have you lost anything, Jacqueline?

1st GIRL. Perhaps her parasol, her gold watch, her smelling-bottle, her little white poodle-dog?

JACQUELINE. You are laughing at me. But— I beg the lady's pardon for interrupting her—but (*to* MISS CHIPPINS) I think, ma'am, you made a mistake.

CATARINA (*aside*). Surely, I should know that voice!

MISS CHIPPINS. I made a mistake, child? How?

JACQUELINE. I found in the collection you made for me, a *gold* piece. Thinking some one must have put it in by mistake for a penny, I have brought it back. Here it is.

MISS CHIPPINS. My good girl, keep it. 'T was mine; I meant it for what it is. (*Turning to* CATARINA.) Would you have looked for so much honesty, Madame, in one so humble and poor.

CATARINA. Yes, for the poor are sometimes the most honest. The gold of the morning sky falls alike on the monarch's throne and the poor man's hovel; and so does the light of probity illume the humblest human heart!

2d GIRL (*aside*). Service has begun!

JACQUELINE (*aside*). That voice! that look! The dignity of that gesture! They seem to recall the unforgotten spell of my childhood!

CATARINA. Come here, girl—here is some more money to add to your purse. (JACQUELINE *approaches*.) Gracious powers! the promptings of my heart did not deceive me; it is indeed *she!*

2d GIRL (*aside*). By Rider Haggard!

MISS CHIPPINS. She! To whom do you refer?

CATARINA. Oh, Jacqueline—my own dear sister Jacqueline! (*Embraces* JACQUELINE.)

JACQUELINE. You know my name?

CATARINA. What! have you forgotten me, Jacqueline? Have time, and care, and the bitter years of our separation effaced all remembrance of Lisette—your sister Lisette, who with you roamed among the hills,

and plucked the flowers from the dell, and gambolled by many a maundering stream in old Savoy?

2d GIRL. I did n't think they were gamblers!

JACQUELINE (*to* CATARINA). Ah, I know you now! You are my own dear, long-lost sister, Lisette!

CATARINA. My dearest Jacqueline!

JACQUELINE. My dearest Lisette! (*They embrace fervently.*)

(1st *and* 2d GIRLS *embrace also, comically.*)

MISS CHIPPINS. This is indeed a singular incident. Young ladies, our presence here is a hindrance to the sisterly joys of those so long severed and now happily reunited! Let us leave them together.

1st GIRL. Yes, come. Who would have expected such a happy meeting!

2d GIRL. I always said there was something distinguished in that flower-girl!

3d GIRL. You did n't!

2d GIRL. I did!

1st GIRL. How can you tell such whoppers!

ANOTHER GIRL. She's all right. Come off!

2d GIRL (*to* 3d). You're a common-minded person!

(*The girls leave the stage wrangling and gossiping.* MISS CHIPPINS *follows.*)

CATARINA. My dear sister, to think that you should be selling flowers, and wandering about, while I was reveling in riches! But I sought you, high and low. Two years ago, when I received my appointment as *prima donna* at La Scala Theatre, I journeyed into Savoy, but only to find our parents dead, our old home broken up, and you gone to tempt fortune in unknown parts.

JACQUELINE. And I, too, have sought you, sister, and vainly. For who could recognize Lisette, of our village, in the famous Donna Catarina, the first singer of the time!

CATARINA. Ah, I remember the hour that made me so. It was at Rome, where our relation Antonio, who is at the Papal Court, procured me an appearance. It was a trying but a glorious ordeal, my first appearance on the stage. They said a tear glistened in my voice that night, for I could not but think of Savoy.

# No. 5. THE TEAR-DROPS IN MINE EYES.

### DUET.

*Allegro moderato.*

CATARINA. *con express.*

The tear-drops in mine eyes were stand - ing, For I was far from old Sa - voy, But still my tim-id heart . . . com-mand - ing, I sang, and feign'd a song of joy! My lay was on - ly bal - lad old - en, And wild as wind   on   moun - tain   brow;      Such rhymes we sang      at sun - set

*ril.*

gold - en,   In days gone by,      remember'st thou?

JACQUELINE.

The songs of old for - get      I    nev - - er, Tho' thro' the

world   com-pell'd   to   roam;      Friend from dear friend dark fate . . .   may sev - er, But ne'er the heart from dream of home! I hear a-

gain the pipe and ta - - bor On mountain peak, in low - ly

dell, The voice of peas - ant freed from la - bor, My heart the

song re-mem-bers well! Come from the

*Giocoso.*

ff p (*Savoyard melody.*)

hills,        come from the      val - leys, Bring with you      dan - ces, mu - sic and

rhyme. Mer - ri - ly dance, cheer - i - ly  sing, And see that ye  keep the prop - er

( *She dances.* )

time!    Tra la la      la,        tra la la  la,      Tra la la -

la,      tra la la  la,      Mer - ri - ly   dance,      cheer - i - ly sing, And see that ye keep the prop - er time! Then come, oh come, come from the

hills, And bring your dan - ces, mu - sic and rhyme, And dance and sing,    mer - ri - ly

sing, And see  ye  keep the  prop - er time! Then dance, . .    mer - ri - ly

dance! And  sing, . .    cheer - i - ly sing!         Sis - ter, was it

CATARINA.

so?      Did our song thus go?      Sis - ter dear, 't was so!   't was

*Un poco meno mosso.*

e - ven so!

Yes, 't is the air, to me en-thrall - ing, Bring-ing back

youth and joys that are fled; Blithe-ly the herd wind - eth his horn, While the flocks an - swer from the shed. Come from the

hills, come from the val - ley, Bring with you dan - ces mu - sic and

rhyme, Mer - ri - ly dance, Cheer - i - ly sing, And see that ye

JACQUELINE.

keep the pro - per time! Then come, oh come, come from the

hills! And bring your dan - ces, mu - sic and rhyme, And dance and

sing, mer - ri - ly sing. And see ye keep the prop - er

time! Then dance, . . mer - ri - ly dance! And sing, . . . cheer-i - ly

Then dance, mer - ri - ly dance! And sing, cheer-i - ly

f
sing. La . . . . . . . . . . . . la la . . . . . . . . . . .
f
sing. La . . . . . . . . . . . . la la . . . . . . . . . . .
f
pp
la . . . . . . . . . . . . . la la . . . . . . . . . . . . . la la la la la la
pp
la . . . . . . . . . . . . . la la . . . . . . . . . . . . . la la la la la la
pp
f
p
la . . la la la la la la la . . la la la la la la
p
la . . la la la la la la la . . la la la la la la
p

la  la  la  la  la  la  la  la  la la  la la  la

la  la  la  la  la  la  la  la la  la la  la

la  la  la . . . . . . . . . . . . . . . . . . . . . . . .

la  la  la . . . . . . . . . . . . . . . . . . . . . . . .

ff

JACQUELINE. And so you sang only the simple songs of our fatherland?

CATARINA. At first. But soon I learned more pretentious songs, — ballads, romances, serenades, even operatic airs. At length a noble lady was so far interested in my voice as to accord me her patronage, her protection. Under the Ægis of her fostering care I matriculated in art and graduated as a full-blown *prima donna*.

JACQUELINE. *Prima donna.*

CATARINA. At La Scala. I am now the reigning celebrity here, as well. But your own story, little one; tell me how *you* have fared ere this.

JACQUELINE. I? Oh, I have but a simple story to tell: my life has been uneventful enough; neither adventure nor fame has chequered its lowly course.

## No. 6.   AH! MINE'S A SIMPLE STORY.

### ROMANCE.

*Allegro moderato assai.*   JACQUELINE.

Ah! mine's a sim - ple sto - - ry . .

. . . Which a thous - and can tell, . . . With tale of love or

glo - ry . . . No ear can I spell, . . . With tale of love or

*colla parte.*

glo - ry No ear . . can I spell!

For when I say I la - bor'd From morn-ing un - to
birds a-mong the branch - es, The flowers a-mong the

night, And of - ten sore - ly hun - ger'd, My tale is told you quite.
grass, Looked all so bright and hap - py, And I so sad, a - las!

Up - on my straw couch dreaming, I slept a-way my
Yet, tho' my life was lone - ly, and light but sel-dom

pain, . . But at the break of morn - ing, I woke to care a - gain! Ah!
shone, . . In heav'n I still con - fid - ed, And hope that led me on! Ah!

*colla parte.*

mine's a sim-ple sto - ry . . Which a thous-and can tell, . . With tale of love or

glo - ry, . . No ear can I spell! With tale of love or glo - ry, No

*colla parte.*

*rit. assai.* *a tempo.* *D.S.*

ear . . can I spell!

2. The

*D.S.*

CATARINA. And we shall part again?

JACQUELINE. Never? How glad I am!

CATARINA. I have earned enough to support us both. With me you will be happy.

JACQUELINE. And together we will revisit Savoy.

CATARINA (*calling to the girls*). Come in, good people all, and witness our happiness.

(*Re-enter* MISS CHIPPINS *and the girls.*)

CATARINA. Before I take my leave of the stage, I invite you all to the opera-house, and will take no refusal. Now, sister mine, heart to heart we will walk through life's vale together.

## No. 7.      HEART TO HEART.

### FINALE.

*Allegro brillante.*

CATARINA.

Heart to heart, . . . . . heart to heart, . . . . With af -

JACQUELINE.

Heart to heart, . . . . . heart to heart, . . . . With af -

CHORUS OF GIRLS AND MISS CHIPPENS.

Heart to heart,      heart to heart,

fec - tion that's ho - ly and pure! 　　Ne'er to 　part, . . . . ne'er to

fec - tion that's ho - ly and pure! 　　Ne'er to 　part, . . . . ne'er to

Love 　　both 　　ho - ly and pure! 　　Ne'er to 　part,

part . . . . From each oth - er while life shall en - dure!

part . . . . From each oth - er while life shall en - dure! 　　　Tears no

ne'er to part, 　While 　their 　life shall en - dure!

*p*

No I'll wipe .... them a-

more .... shall be flow - - - ing,

way, . . And our hearts shall be grow - ing, In af - fec - - tion each

Yes! . . And our hearts shall be grow - ing, In af - fec - - tion each

*cres.*

day! . . . . . Heart to heart, . . . . heart to heart, . . . . With af-

day! . . . . . Heart to heart, . . . . heart to heart, . . . . With af-

Heart to heart,      heart to heart,

-fec-tion that's ho-ly and pure, . . . . . Ne'er to part, . . . . . ne'er to

-fec-tion that's ho-ly and pure, . . . . . Ne'er to part, . . . . . ne'er to

Love     both     ho-ly and pure,     Ne'er to part,

part . . . . . While our life shall en - dure! While our

part . . . . . While our life shall en - dure! While our

ne'er to part, While their life shall en -

life shall en - dure! While our life shall en -

life shall en - dure! While our life shall en -

dure! While their life shall en - dure! While their

dure! While . . . . . . our life, While . . . . . . our

dure! While . . . . . our life, While . . . . . our

life shall . . . . . . en - - - dure! While . . . . . . their

life shall . . . . . . . en - dure!

life shall . . . . . . en - dure!

life shall . . . . . . . en - dure!

(CURTAIN.)

FINE.

www.ingramcontent.com/pod-product-compliance
Lightning Source LLC
Chambersburg PA
CBHW021642270326
41931CB00008B/1133